CRITICISM

HOW TO TURN YOUR WORST ENEMY TO BEST FRIEND

MAYANK SINGH

To my dear Father and Mother who always taught me importance of virtues in my life .

Love you mom and dad

Contents

Preface

The journey of life is full of many challenges and the way you go ahead in your life and deal with different challenges determines the quality of our life. One challenge which we all come across in our life is criticism and very few people know how to handle it in a way that it become a asset for you . This book provides you with important lesson which will transform the way you deal with the criticism. Words always have power to heal people or to start war between nations. If you are not equipped with right tools to deal with criticism, you will be used by people to get their things done,drain your energy and bring you down from reaching the goals in your life.

Let me tell you a story about the Gautama Buddha, one day Buddha was passing by the village. He sat down near a tree , people started gathering around him and one young men came near him . He started abusing Buddha and also insulting him by saying that you are here for our food and money . Buddha keep on smiling at him and did not utter a single word to him . Man went back to village after hurling abuses at Buddha. That night he was full of remorse and was thinking that why after such harsh words Buddha did not reply . Next day he again reached to the place Buddha was staying. Buddha was giving discourse to people and he came near Buddha and asked him, yesterday I abused you and insulted you but you did not reply why? .Buddha calmly replied dear young man have you ever gifted someone something and if that person refused to take it. Young men replied yes. Then does it belong to you or the person who declined it. Young men replied "to me". That is what exactly happened when you abused me and insulted me I didn't accepted it. Person melted and bow his head in front of Buddha.

What Buddha did is he turned a critique into his follower, we all may not become Buddha, but surely can learn the mindset to change ourselves to deal with criticism in smartest possible way.

Acknowledgements

I am extremely grateful to all the people around me who have taught me the value of support system in life

People who have been part of this are very valuable to me. My sincere thanks to everyone who make it happen . I would like to thanks a very dear friend of mine to whom i am indebited so much "Deeksha jain" . I would like to thanks my brother Arjit for being a support and healthy critique

Prologue

The story of this book begins with the need to make people aware about the real problems of life. Many people are not exposed to it due to living in a closed and safe environments created by our loved ones. When they are exposed all of sudden to this world, it impacts their mental state and mental health in such a way that it have a deep and long lasting impact on them.

Criticism, trolling and now days what we call online trolling has very deep impact on our mental state and many people in today's world are getting heckled by these trollers. Many people go to extreme measures to deal with people others just take abuse and sit silent. We must know how to deal with these people who use criticism to derail you from your path of progress. You have all the right to reach your destiny without being interrupted or getting disturbed by people like these. I request you if you learn a thing or two from this book to deal with criticism please pass it on to others so that we can create more confident individuals and help more and more people to deal with abusive people.

I myself like many others was deeply impacted by it and I really hate and get triggered when I see people in power bullying those who do not have power. But through a Socratic dialogue I was able to figure out the root cause of this problem. My inability to handle criticism acted like a roadblock for many years of my life until I figured out how to win it over and made it my biggest asset which now works only for my benefit.

Now I want to share it with all of you so that you can deal with criticism effectively and can use it as a productivity tool to move forward and faster in life.

1

Introduction

Criticism is something we all are aware of, although the degree to which we deal with it may vary from person to person. Still I would like to define it ,which would make it easier to understand and bring us all on same page to what we call criticism

Criticism according to a dictionary is expression of disapproval of someone or something on the basis of perceived fault or mistakes. The point here to note is "perceived fault or mistake ". If you could understand it ,you are a step higher in dealing with the the criticism . Broadly speaking , anything unpleasant that is being said to us , we may consider it as criticism.

criticism invokes a emotional response in us and thus it should also be considered from angle of emotion . Well their is no denying of the fact that for a normal person, criticism invokes a emotional response and it feels bad when someone say us something unpleasant or even something good in a harsh tone. But how do we react after that or I would say respond after that would determine our ability to handle criticism and our well being .

This is the age of information and the information is flowing at such tremendous rate . If you are on any social media platform you may have come across criticism once in a while. Even at home or your workplace you may often came across heaps of criticism . But if you don't know how to make criticism your friend . You would probably become a victim of criticism . By default criticism is your enemy untill you learn to make it your friend . When you learn this art of converting your enemy into your friend you can grow at very fast rate in your life .

Criticism could best be understood through a example . Conversation is said to be completed when there is some form of feedback . Now that feedback could be considered good or bad by you depending upon how you take it and what your mood and circumstances are. When we are in school , teacher often give us remarks like good , poor , keep it up , can do better , excellent. Teacher said to you that you are a poor student in some subject. Now it is basic feedback which could be considered as criticism . The mistake many of us does is take it so much seriously that it acts as a roadblock in your studies. Student often start ignoring that subject and slowly slowly, it lead to student really becoming poor in that subject.

Look at that statement as a feedback that is based on your performance compared with other students in your class or as per the expectations of the teacher. But the teacher doesn't know the circumstances you are in . May be you were ill or any other issue you were dealing with hampered your performance. But teacher is unaware of that and will not consider that while making any statement on you. Many times teachers are internally biased while grading students and that results in motivating those students more which he think can perform better rather than motivating each and every student and giving special attention and motivation to the student who need it the most. Not many Teachers recognize the impact they can have on mind of young individuals.

Supportive parents and family can help and give their young ones the required confidence to deal with situations they encounter. Role of parents and parenting became very crucial in letting their kids know how good they are and how they need to deal with people and others who bully them in their class, but I guess not many parents take time to go beyond asking the grades of their kids. I urge everyone who can instill confidence in young kids to please do it so that they can deal with criticism, bullying and every other problem of their life effectively.

Remember that what is going to make criticism your friend or enemy is you and how you internalize that statement. If that statement stops you from doing well in studies ,then you must learn to make criticism your friend. Someone might think that this is a very particular example and the level of criticism which they have witnessed was far more critical than this . I totally agree with you that criticism can become very nasty and harsh when it comes from people in power or someone dear and there is no way to retort to it. I will surely go deep into every aspect of criticism and also its sources . One thing that should be kept in mind is that I am not going to tell you or help you turn every critic into your friend. But I am surely going to help you to convert every negative feedback which you receive into a force to drive you further ahead in your life .

I personally had battled with criticism at so many levels in my life and to be precise it was a big enemy for me. When I started understanding it holistically and turned it into my friend, I felt like burden went from my shoulders and I can leap towards my goals much faster rate . I am taking this friendship more further by way of practice and with every feedback (negative or positive) provided to me by others.

The first step towards making it you friend is to reverse the effect of all the criticism which you have received in your life. Either you do it first thing in the morning or just before sleep, lying on the bed whichever time suits you. Count in reverse from ten to one , take atleast 3 deep breaths and then say to yourself or you can write 3 good thing about yourself and keep repeating it daily for at least two months to three months and you will see change in yourself. With this practice the effects that criticism has on you will disappear slowly and eventually you would free yourself from any kind of baggage of criticism you are carrying . You want to do it further or not is entirely upto you.

This exercise clears your mind of criticism you are currently receiving and that you have received till now . Once you worked upon it you are ready to take a deeper down look toward making it our friend as now criticism is no more our enemy . So to know about our friend criticism I have divided it into four parts which we will see one by one to grab an understanding about it .

- *Self criticism*
- *Destructive criticism*
- *Abusive criticism*
- *Constructive criticism*

Let us go back to the part where I said criticism is based on other person's perception of your performance or act. Someone else perception can never Guage into you reality . Person's perception is a very complex construct which is based on their biases, their understanding of the situation and the action around them and your behavior towards them .You need to understand that the best purpose criticism can serve is to act as a cue for you to know about your mistakes and find out the scope of improvement . Never let other people opinion and criticism take a driver seat in your life. It should act as a fuel(cue) for you to move further in your life .

2

Self Criticism

Self criticism is evaluating a particular situation or event in one's life and the cue obtained from other people feedback. This lead to creation of internal thoughts (mostly negative). Which can lead to self doubt and impede one's progress in life. Let us start from self evaluation and see how healthy striving which is self focused is different from being overly self critical which is a negative personality trait in psychology.

We all have tendency to self evaluate our personality, physical appearances ,behaviour, actions, emotions and also how we reacted in a particular situation. This evaluation gives us cues about which area to work upon and which area to ignore ,we get an insight about our strength and our weakness. Being overly critical we often tend to overlook and underlay our strengths and magnify our weakness by thinking about it over and over again. If we keep on internalizing on wrong cues put forward by others or ourself . It could become biggest handicap in our life. Overly self critical person evaluate each and every action and word that he speak and thereby this takes so much of his mental space and energy that it deprives him of all the good places and event where he could have invested that energy.

This leads to creation of a self reinforcing cycle in the life of the person which starts with negative thoughts and ends at high probability of failure. Negative thoughts creates self doubt in person which leads to under confident action and it results in high probability of failure

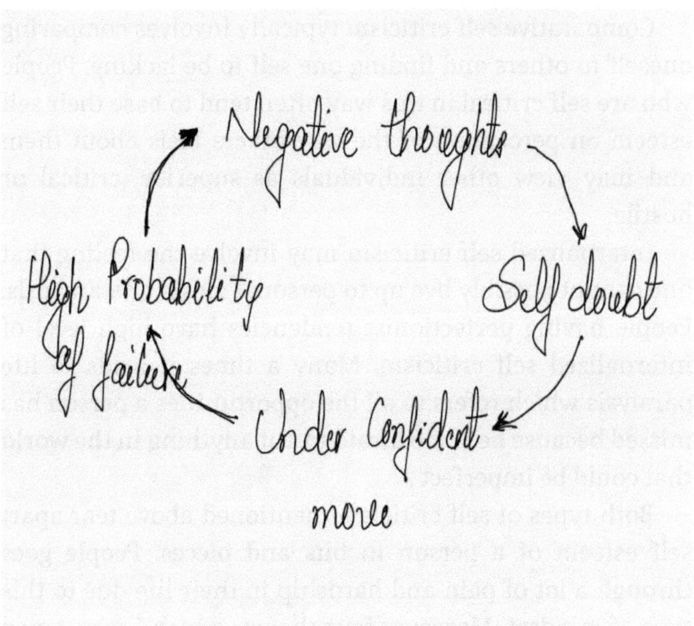

It makes the person less assertive and he becomes people pleaser so as to avoid being hurted . Mental well being of the person is severely affected. Four main themes which are generally noticed in self criticism are

- Being harsh or strict with yourself

- Feeling guilt or angry
- Feeling useless or like a burden
- Feeling ashamed and not wanting to show weakness

Many people have worked upon in pschology to understand the ill effects of self criticism . One of study by Thompson and Zuroff talk about two types of self criticism

A. Comparative B. Internalized

Comparative self criticism typically involves comparing oneself to others and finding one self to be lacking. People who are self critical in this way often tend to base their self esteem on perception of the way others feels about them and may view other individuals as superior ,critical or hostile.

Internalized self criticism may involve the feeling that one cannot possibly live up to personal ideals or standards. People having perfectionist tendencies have high level of internalized self criticism. Many a times it leads to life paralysis which refers to all the opportunities a person has missed because he is too afraid to put anything in the world that could be imperfect .

Both types of self criticism mentioned above tear apart self esteem of a person in bits and pieces. People goes through a lot of pain and hardship in their life due to this type of mindset. Moreover four themes which I mentioned before keep on taking more and more stronger form with time. In more extreme form it can also lead to isolating tendencies ,escapism,depression.

We have to move towards healthy striving which is focused on moving forward using feedback without being affected by it . In order to reach this spectrum of self criticism we have to develop a healthy mindset which is spun by self love or self compassion , being easy towards life or having a sense of humor about oneself and confidence about one's strength .

Self love + Sense of humor about oneself + confidence in one's strength

We can develop each of them in our life . It is just a matter of practice . I would also like to mention that if you are having support system with you it will accelerate your progress journey . Even if you do not have right support system you can develop it on your own.

For a person to have confidence in his strength , he first need to find them. Many of us have not realized their true potential yet . But to find your strength and bring some purpose out of it requires your time and effort. One of the way to find it is self introspection. You need to sit alone without any devices ,without any external interference. Try to recollect things that you enjoyed as a kid and take a note of it on a paper. Then find qualities or skill that you enjoy and are good at ,list is narrowed down . Use this list to find any job which is already available that satisfy your criteria and you can earn from it . The earning potential of job adds confidence in us, but most important part is we must enjoy atleast 80 percent of task related to the job. If there is some part of our job that we don't like or do not enjoy it is okay but we must enjoy atleast 80 percent of it . There will always be part of your job that you may not like but in order to enjoy that 80 percent you need to do that 20 percent which you don't like because it is necessary . If no job is available that suits your criteria then you need to invent ways to use you skills in a way it benefit the society which will create the earning potential . The process can be done step by step . Once you have found your strength then you have to repeat it untill you start gaining confidence and with time your strengths will start bearing fruit .

A person who is secure about his strength can take humor about himself and has ability to laugh about himself . By doing so he becomes light in his attitude. Taking jokes on you, doesn't make you lesser or weaker . It only shows that you are secure enough to laugh at your weaker areas. When you will laugh at your mistakes ,it will take out a lot of stress from your life.

Self compassion is much needed in today's times when everyone around you is having a shallow interaction with each other and on basis of that shallow interaction people are mud slinging on each others qualities performance,personality. Self compassion can become your best friend . It can become your best remedy in tough times . It springs up from forgiveness and grows from accepting yourself the way you are . You might have set some parameter for yourself to achieve and you haven't even reached the halfway mark but you still need to have compassion and love and respect for your efforts that you have taken . You should not compare yourself with the other person . Why ? Because it is your journey and you have all the right to take on your journey in the way you want. Be your own light and be your own guide .

People only value the results that have come in the real world . But the process of self compassion teach you to value your efforts which may not bore any fruits today. You have to very soft while dealing with yourself during tough times . Being more critical will only stop you from going forward in area of success. Remember that you can run away from every person in the world but cannot run away from yourself. So when you have this attitude of being overly analytical and criticize yourself at failing at something or getting something, your mind in order to avoid pain of self criticism will try to avoid things where you are not good at or you fail in those things

Love is a wonderful feeling ,when we are feeling loved , it is very special and beautiful experience which is beyond ordinary words to describe. Our whole existence start to come in front of us and we act and talk with more confidence . Our actions become more pleasant and we see more goodness in everyone. Our perception of reality is tilted more towards the rosy side. Self love spring up from self compassion towards ourself . We tend to look more towards our positive qualities than towards our mistake and our optimism towards life and people increases. Similarly our trust and love in almighty god or the universe has same sort of magical effect on us. Growth of science lead to rationalization of concept of religion and confirmation of religious principle with the science . It become so important that it lead to our decreasing belief in the existence of God. I will not tell you to believe or to question the existence of God. But I want to tell you that believing in the god or universe surely gave us more faith in life. It give us ability to withstand tough times .

Self love is important in today's time as it leads you to become the best version of yourself. You have infinite potential in yourself and it is your duty to find ways to let it manifest in the world . I am sure that each and everyone of you who is reading this will find it and I really believe in your choices and decision and value your efforts to overcome roadblocks in your life.

3

Destructive Criticism

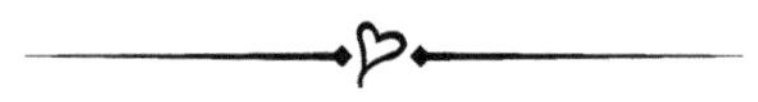

Destructive criticism is when someone abuses you or criticize you in order to bring you down ,hurt you emotionally mentally and there is not a single path to make it a chance of improvement. we must understand that this type of criticism is most destructive in terms of impact

Let us take an example to understand ,A person say to another person that you can't be an intelligent person because you belong to an certain race . When someone usually make an extreme statement regarding you and rather than pointing your mistake it is destructive in nature . Few examples are

- you can never achieve this thing .
- You do not have ability to get anything in your life
- You are a bad person

Moreover the way someone delivers that feedback make it way more destructive. But you have to remember the moment you accept it you become a victim of criticism and make criticism your enemy .In later chapter I will also tell you how to deliver a negative message such that it might not hurt even the most sensitive soul .

Destructive criticism is generally meant to hurt someone . But many of the times speaker is unaware of the disastrous impact their criticism have on others. First step is to identify that in this criticism there is no element, where you can find positive ray of light . The examples that I have mentioned above that you can never get thing in your life is a statement which tells you that you stop the pursuit . It will be said to demotivate you from getting those thing which others do not want you to achieve or they themselves think are impossible to achieve . If it is said that , it is very hard to get this thing then it becomes a totally different statement which still have element of hope.

Now that you know that this criticism is destructive in nature then you have to separate the emotion that is attached to that message . If you do this part you just snatch the power of your critic at the very moment . But many of us cannot do it . It is okay to not feel good in that moment and you may keep continue to feel bad for a certain time depending upon your level of sensitivity and proximity to the person who is delivering you the message. If the message is delivered by someone who is very dear to you it becomes very fatal and in some cases it leads you to take disastrous step.

We should know that feedback which is destructive in nature is meant to limit your potential and to make you react in way that disturbs your wellbeing . We react to destructive criticism because of emotion and the intention that is being attached to it . Letting the emotion of speaker invoke in you an unwanted emotion will not serve you any purpose to deal with it . The intent of speaker will meant a lot for you because that is only way you know who to trust and which person is not trustworthy .

Destructive criticism is generally repetitive in nature till the speaker obtain the desire objective to abstain you from doing something or any other hidden agenda. It is not necessary that a person would say same words again . But somehow the meaning and area of target will remain same . It leads you to ultimately give up and accept it as a reality . If you notice carefully some of our boundaries are actually created because of response or feedback of people around us . Destructive criticism is used to create superficial boundaries for you or drop you down to a lower level you already are.

The message is loud and clear . There is no way you can be letting a person who is delivering you the a destructive message again and again hurt you . Now what is the ideal way out to such a critic and this type of criticism . Never let the emotion of critic sweep inside you . Let me tell you through a example . When someone is cursing you and in your mind you are saying God bless this idiot and outer appearance is a light smile . This type of gesture is enough to destroy your enemy or person who is delivering the destructive message .

Now to make it easy we must also identify what is source of feedback

1. Someone near and dear (family,partner)
2. Person who is your friend or you know(friends and relatives)
3. Person who you do not know

If a person doesn't know you and delivers you a destructive message than you must ignore him and say to him in your mind "God give him some mind ". It will release the bad emotions and energy which is being generated in you due to his negative feedback . Addressing the person will only deprive you of your energy and time and this is what that person might actually might have wanted . Mostly people on internet and many people who know you from very far and very less, fall in this category . Explaining them or replying them will only entangle you more . Leave it right there and ignore it .

If that person is your friend , it becomes necessary for you to tell him how you feel regarding his/her negative feedback and that conversation should be done as soon as possible to avoid any misunderstanding to let your friendship intact. If that person is part of your family or any very important person in your life then use tool of patience and try to make them understand about everything patiently . But if still things doesn't goes well. Then please do not shy away from creating gap between you and your critic at different level . Afterwards you will know what was really hurting you and eventually you can take a decision . Thing to remember here is that we must never force ourselves to live unhappy because if we are happy then only we can make a happy world.

4

Abusive Criticism

Sometimes, criticism is done not to inflict long term wounds but for discouraging some behavior or action which other person may consider to be wrong . Let us take an example people troll many women for wearing a revealing dress . Each person has its own parameter of a revealing dress and they criticize others on basis of that . Abusers never think of any argument from others point of view they just think that their view is the the ultimate view and troll or abuse others on basis of that parameter.

We must understand that this type of criticism becomes effective only when we become discouraged even when we were doing thing in right way . We must not let the critic affect us in way that it become an hindrance in achieving our goal .Abusive criticism can become severe if it is combined with both soft or hard emotions . As hard emotions like anger generates fear and self doubt . Soft emotions generate dilemma and feeling of guilt .Thus it leads you to be coerced into some decision or path which may not have desired for .

You loose the battle even if you try to clear every issue or every event to each and every troller or critic . There may be times when it is absolutely critical to clear the issue as it is sensitive then only give a reply otherwise just do not waste energy into replying a troller or critic which you may encounter across. There is famous saying that" never drop your sword but don't use it frequently ". You have pretty good thing to do in life, focus on them . Moreover if the critic is intending to discourage you, the best slap you can give him is the slap of ignorance . More attention you pay ,more powerful critic becomes. It is your life You do not own any explanation to others .

Here also you can divide on basis of source of feedback

1. Someone you know
2. Someone you don't know

If it is someone you don't know and they criticize you in a abusive manner then you have two options depending upon area they are entering into , if they are entering into your personal space you may choose to give them a befitting reply . But if it is not your personal space you may ignore them ideally and if you wish you ,as reply but only depending upon sensitivity of the issue .

If it is someone you know then you need to observe , may be it is due to bad day or bad mood they are getting irrated with thing they usually don't and want you to behave in a particular manner . But if it is said with or delivered in not so pleasant manner . Wait for sometime and then make them understand that this is not the way they can treat you . You have to show the world the right way to treat you . You have all the right to be treated with dignity and respect . Never ever let anyone snatch it from you .

5

Constructive criticism

In this section we are going to talk about what is constructive criticism it's role in our personal improvement and how to deliver a message or criticize that other person receive it without any resistance and without getting hurt .

When the feedback is interpreted as trying to say something bad but leaves a trail of improvement then it is considered as constructive criticism . Constructive criticism can be used as a tool of improvement and it is the only form of criticism which should be welcomed with open arms rather than being discarded . It is generally intended to made other person uncomfortable , so that they can become more better .

We must be open to this form of criticism. Let me tell you a story there was a group of monkey who were shivering in cold . They catch a firefly and one of the monkey was trying to blow it and others were keenly watching and cheering him up . They would have seen humans blow a dry wood chips for generating fire . A wise bird was sitting on a nearby tree and watching all this happening in front of him . She advised them " dear friend you are doing wrong thing, don't blow it". It is a firefly ,it will not burn . It is the wood that burns" . But they refused to accept the advice of bird saying you have a small brain don't you dare advice us. They keep on blowing the firefly and shivering all night. Moral of the story is wise advice even in the form of criticism can save you from wasting your time , energy and efforts.

We must acknowledge the constructive criticism and let us go a bit further in journey of improvement . Even if we do not agree with the person, an honest introspection will not do any harm to us . Many business take it as a pivotal point in their journey of improvement. Feedback from customer can prove crucial to health of any company or business. Many people desire constructive feedback from other as seen in a latest research by American Psychological association but they themselves are afraid to give constructive feedback from the fear of being judged or it may be viewed as negative feedback. We must understand that constructive feedback is really important for us and other to fast track on the path of progress. We are limited in our perspective from which we look at ourselves and others. So feedback can also serve the purpose of enhancing our perspective from others point of view. Feedback is an important tool in our life if we know how to use it correctly and efficiently.

Now what if we want to deliver a negative statement to other person. what is right way of delivering it to people, so that they doesn't get hurt. Please remember the way you say a thing or the manner you say is more important than the words you choose. Your way of delivering a negative message should be gentle and firm. It should not be abusive or harsh tone in which you deliver the message . After this comes the choice of words . You need to keep on working on the choice of words throughout your life . There will always be some scope of improvement in this area.

Let us take a situation. In a office a new office workers who is good at work is being late consequtively from last four days . His senior instead of scolding him ,can deliver message in a completely different manner. He can say " his name,you are really working hard for our company and started to get along with everyone in the office . I did appreciate if you start coming early on time . I wish you don't have any problem in coming on time. Do you? . Most probably his answers would be in positive and he will make commitment from his side rather than being enforced by you . So you must never run away from delivering any negative feedback as it is a chance for another person to improve .

6

Trolling

I would like to share with you personal incidents of criticism which I encountered in my life. My early encounter with criticism was when I was a kid i was always scolded by my mom for getting 2nd rank or 3rd rank in class. My mother always wanted me to come first in class , coming second was not at all accepted. But mostly I was loved by everyone and a obedient guy no one usually criticize for doing anything out of the way. I became rebellious when I came in college and was questioning everything around me and was experimenting with many things which let me earn a lot of criticism along with praise.

One incident I still remember of collegetime, I was working with a NGO working to clean the city. We clean public places which are used so much and are covered with posters and lots of others stuff. One day when I was cleaning the wall one of my friend took my picture and put it on social media . I was wearing a mask as I had allergy due to dust . It received a lot of praise but I stuck on a comment which says shame on young people who try to hide their face while cleaning our country's public places instead of taking pride in it . I cannot believe that there was a person who was commenting on my picture like this . Maybe if criticism was my friend I may not have reacted the way I reacted on it and I would not be worried about it . But at that time I was not accustomed of trolling . I felt very bad due to that comment as I was trying to do something good for my society and I did not like people judging it like that .

After that feeling bad for two three days , I messaged him through my brother's account as I don't have one account back then . I explained him my condition in a very detailed manner and he after 12 days replied to me OK. He just don't care about me or anything else and I wasted so much time energy and effort just to make him understand my reality . Now , when criticism is my friend I know how I should have dealt with him back then . I hope everyone in today's time will become educated on how to handle criticism . So they would not need to endure pain due to others insensitive attitude.

Every year many people become victim of trolling and with the surge of social media platform which give trolls a safe and a hideous den from where they can attack on their prey . Trolls usually say bad and offensive thing about other people whom they target . Trolling can have a objective or maybe it might not have any objective . Trollers usually target our vulnerability and comment on things we are emotionally attached . According to a survey in 2019 trolling has become so common that one in three people have experienced some form of online trolling like threats , abusive language , unsolicited images on internet. People from different fields have experienced it and became victim of these trolls . One of the celebrated gymnast Simone biles talked about effect of faceless trolls on his mental health. You might have heard the name of a TV presenter of Australia Charlotte Dawson who committed suicide because of online trolling. Trolling can not brushed off as something you can avoid or say that I will not face it. Every person need to understand about the trolling and how to diffuse even the biggest troller you may come across in your life or online.

I also like to say that not every troller is a monster who is unleased for hurting other people , sometimes trollers are people who do not have anything to hang on in their life and sad people who want to make other people sad.

In order to deal with the troller you need to remember word DAP . DAP stands for detterence,attention,prevention. Let's us see how can you create a DAP system in order to deal with the trollers. First is detterence which means trollers should always be aware of consequences of crossing a certain boundary that you have set . The instilled fear in other people stops them from crossing the boundaries in case of an argument and while you are replying to something . A credible detterence can also be set up by showing that you can take strict actions even when you have no idea of using them . Every social media platform have a system where you can report the trollers instead of engaging them . Moreover every country have some form of legal safeguard against trolling which goes at nasty level . You need to know the safeguards which are available in you country which will help you in case the trollers goes out of hand .

Second is Attention, Every troller is like a parasite which feeds on the victims attention, the more attention people give him more powerful it grows. You should take atmost care that you are not giving him any attention until and unless you think that it should necessarily be addressed to a larger group of people.The moment you rob them of attention you are making the troller weaker and they will also be demotivated to further carry on this activity.

Third is prevention, prevention is done by taking real measures which prevents others from entering your territory. Let us say you engage with unknown person in a discussion but the moment it turn toxic you stop debating with the person . Allowing only healthy comments on the site or post that you upload filtering or auto deleting or manually removing hate comments .Such measures let other know what your boundaries are and you make them clearly visible to everyone. You can even apply this system to any troll you come across in real life.

7

Social criticism

Social criticism according to Wikipedia is form of academic or journalistic criticism on sociological issues in contemporary society,in particular with respect to perceived injustice and power relation . Every society has some issues at local level and same is true for state level , national level and international level. Each and every society has scope of improvement and so does its old social structures which are rusted over time. A nation's collective thinking ,desires, aspiration change over time as the people change over time. These changes come from different sociological ,economical and ever changing circumstances of our society.

The proper question is what is the proper use of criticism in a society. It should not be used as tool to demean each others differences and comparing these differences to belittle each other. It should be used as a tool to create a sustainable impact rather than disastrous result on a individual level or to a society.

Social criticism can be of two types one is more sort of bringing into your knowledge where does the problem exist and another one is the one in which we also offer some form of solution to it and collective discussion and deliberation will eventually improve the solution , making it more sustainable and relevant to a particular problem.

Let us take an issue which exist at international level is pollution and climate change. Whole world is facing the consequences of the changing enviornment due to pollution and Many of the world leaders and government are ignorant about it . Many of leaders are atmost showing at global forum or meeting that they are concerned . But on ground their is much which needs to be done. We as a society are not enough critical of the actions taken by our government for saving our mother nature. They keep on deceiving us that this bargain to sacrifice our nature is necessary in the name of creating a false sense of progress and security.

Many environmental activist are working in this field to bring our notice the impact of pollution is having on the quality of life. We must also see and become critical of any unsustainable practice which may be part of our lifestyle or our society. These practice can be part of society for very long time , many of these practices can also be religious in nature and that also need to be challenged. Many religion of the world are self evolving in this sense to adapt according to the changing needs of our mother earth. Many people are adapting to practices which are resulting in having lesser carbon footprint.

We must never shy away in bringing to notice such practice which are unsustainable to our nature and society. By being critical of such practices we are going to transform our enviornment step by step and leading to a society with habit of coexisting with nature rather than fighting with it. Many people want to challenge such social structure but limit themselves to not being more vocal about it due to the backlash that can come on it. As a society we need to create safe atmosphere for people to voice their opinion without hurting others. Artistic expression and a touch of humor can help while we are criticizing any sort of flawed social structure and delivering message in this way is less offending to those that sit in power. We can take different type of action steps at individual level which will ultimately lead us to be more vocal about more pressing issues that exist in our society.

Many a times we come across about news of racial abuse in many of the countries. Although they are trying to integrate at economic level, but people to people integration is still lacking . Racial abuse still exist in many society is not a hidden issue . Even these type of practices can make society a bad place to live. In many Asian countries problems exist due to lack of integration of people of different religion and region and linguistic diffrences. We must understand as a society plurality of thoughts and ideas is a healthy thing. Plurality of ideas helps us in many many ways and thus maintains a healthy balance in the society. we can take some inspiration from nature. Nature is so diverse and each element plays a part or role in it . We never find diversity of nature is acting as a negative influence it is always an positive influence. Thus we can see the use and importance in a broad manner rather than using in a bad way can help create a better society

8

Healthy boundaries

Boundaries are the intermittent junction where one thing ends and other thing start. Our skin is a boundary in that sense. Countries have a well defined boundary. So boundaries have a two fold purpose . First is to define or differentiate one thing from other and another is to hold certain amount of things together. There are some natural boundaries and also certain boundaries which are man made to live their life in more organized manner. We have made many boundaries in the world which are irrelevant and thus tend to be destroyed. I must say that I am not a huge advocate of drawing boundaries which are very much impermeable.

Now let us see how we can introduce the concept of boundaries so that it turn criticism into our friend . We till now has learned that not all criticism is bad. There is some form of criticism which we can use to become better. But you might have thought that to let each and every feedback and process is time taking or boring . The concept of healthy boundaries is to make simple for you to choose which message or feedback should be accepted and which is to be discarded.

We must define in our life who are our wellwishers and are concerned about us and who are people who are just there to hangout and have fun with you . If you want to know how are people who take your life towards growth. You should reflect upon your life and see if there are people who genuinely happy when you win and who considers your pain as their pain. Then these are the people whose feedback is worth considering. I am not saying to accept each and every piece of their advice. But you must accept their advice that have substance and which will help you to become better.

There is something you should know before deciding whose advice you can take. Not everyone near you can and related to you can give you the best piece of advice. Let me tell you about Mr Amitabh Bachchan, when he decided to do Indian version of show who want to be a millionaire many people adviced him not do that as it will affect his stardom.Even his own family adviced him against doing the show. Although they did not force him not to do the show. But it was his own call to do the show disregarding the advice given to him by most of the people. So you must always be your first well wisher before adding anyone to the list. Everyone have some of their biases and these biases impact their decision making which then reflect in their advice.

Now you do not need to filter every feedback thrown at you. You may have to consider people who are really concerned about you.You can use the method of filtering to process their advice. You can make a boundary under which their are people whose advice is worth considering and moreover this boundary is dynamic , with change of time and circumstance you can choose whether people who are inside should remain in or when you should bring anyone in this boundary. The concept of keeping it dynamic is what makes it a healthy boundary. Many people those who have boundaries end up making economic chamber which validates their own views and thoughts . Eco chambers will present a reality which is one sided and you will never be able to see big picture. People interest change with time and also their goals keep updating with time . Keeping boundary dynamic also allows you to throw out people which you have once included on basis of having mutual interest, but with time one of you have changed their interest.

9

Installing a filter

Filter is something which purifies a thing and give us a useful output while taking out the unwanted part. As you know by now that not all criticism is bad. But we only need the good part of criticism, and don't want the bad part of it to affect us. There are two parts which are basically used in developing a filter which will make you endure the bad and accept the good which comes out of filtration. Acceptance part we will talk about that later . Here we will take the part of enduring the unfiltered which contains the good and bad. We will also talk about how to throw the bad part and let the good part percolate down. Let me tell you a story which will tell you how to endure criticism and thus you can laugh off bad part and accept the good part.

My uncle came to our house to visit my father who was ill. I was there and my uncle started saying to me that you don't care about father as i don't have his previous ailments history saved. My father rarely got ill. So it never crossed our mind to save his history. But I patiently clarified him and he immediately say that I have all my son's history saved in a file . Well I thought it's a good idea to stack patients history. I validated his idea and he transformed from being angry to become happy while explaining the process of doing it. You can see that I took what was good and discarded what was bad. Moreover I handled in a ver matur. e manner . It was all because my endurance to criticism was very high now which was very low back when I was a kid. If my endurance to criticism was low, I may have pointed out fingers at him rather than dealing in a more mature manner.

Endurance to criticism is developed with time or we can proactively develop it by interacting with more and more people . My brother has very high endurance for criticism and he does this very crazy activity to develop his muscle of endurance to criticism. He go to social media and does a comment which is usually against the flow and endure the criticism which comes from different people with grace. I must tell you he doesn't hurt anyone but challenges the general perception. One day a comment was written A CA work hardest to become CA and no one can compete with the hardworking of CA. All the others CA were writing below it true , so correct etc. He commented bellow doctors work that much in a year that CA does in a year and after that he was enjoying the criticism which came after it because he really did not believe that any work from different field can be compared. He just want to have some fun and just wrote bless you to even the worst form of criticism he received.

My message is not to tell you to do the same. I want to tell you that going out facing people you develop your muscle of endurance and tolerance rather than being isolated. Once your endurance muscle is developed you can take even the harsh comments with grace. After this you must decide that what is constructive in this criticism and take a note of it. To accept or not is another issue but at least let the constructive part percolate down and take a mental note of it or write it ,whatever seems suitable to you. Here I want to share with you story of (Crickter)Sachin Tendulkar . Sachin met guruprasad a hotel staffer at the Taj coriander in Chennai who gave him a crucial advice on his elbow guard and his bat swing . Guruprasad told Sachin how his elbow guard was affecting his full swing movement and Sachin asked him how did he know that he told Sachin that he had observed it in TV. Sachin instead of brushing it as a advice or feedback from a laymen took a mental note of it and it led to making some changes which really helped him improve his game. Sachin open handed attitude towards that advice helped him. Similarly we can remain open handed to criticism and let us propel towards excellence.

10

Turning criticism your friend

The hardest part of making criticism your friend is to accept and change. In our life we ran away from accepting that something is wrong in the way we are doing things and to change either for better or worse. We like to maintain a status quo in our life. Even if we change then that thought should be completely ours not of someone who is advising us. People,events and the experiences of others can help in initiateing the thoughts which will led you to realize that change is needed in your life.

We must understand that acceptance and change are for our betterment not of other. If someone say you are fat and he is body shaming you then he is absolutely wrong at that time. But you are overweight and your parent are asking you to exercise out of their concern they are not abusing you or bullying you. I hope you must understand that it is out of concern and not anything else. But you should not be taking or accepting every advice that you came across. You might have heard about story of salt trader and mule. If not, let me tell you A salt trader father and his fourteen year old son are travelling from one place to another carrying load of salt on his mule. After walking some distance father says to his son that you may be tired you can sit on mule for some rest. After walking few steps some passerby comment that what a unworthy son,father is standing and he is sitting on the mule.Son feels bad and comes down and ask his father to ride on the mule. Father sits on the mule. After travelling some more distance , few passerby cross them while commenting how shameful that a father is sitting on the mule and letting his son stand in such harsh weather. Father got affected by these comments and now both sit on the mule. After walking some ,ore distance they came across another batch of people who confront them both and say how inhumane you are you might kill this animal by sitting on him. Then reacting to their comments both of them come on the ground and start walking by and again a farmer walk by who comment how foolish people are these inspite of having a mule they are walking on foot.

Moral of the story you must not change just because your society or others want it but you should take the challenge to change if you really want it and it's for betterment. When you make a mental note to something you are doing which can be done in a more better way than do make change in yor way to make it better. But final call sholuld always be yours which is unaffected by the biases of society and even your own biases should be placed apart.

Let me tell you about another tool you can use to fight criticism. Positive misinterpretation means actually you use criticism thrown at you in fun and a positive way. Let us say some people say you are stubborn in a bad sense. You can reply yeah I am because stubbornness is what it takes to change the world.

If you have understood what I have said till now then you ,use have understood criticism have potential to be your friend . Please repeat it I hereby declare from now on criticism is my good friend and it will always help me to become better rather than hurting me . With this declaration going into your mind, criticism is officially your friend from now on and it can never harm you in any way. Now you have power to laugh at your mistakes making your critic armless and living your life in a way that is immune to any kind of abuse . Your mind has certain role to play in making this belief as truth,till then just have it as a belief and soon it will be truth. Slowly as time pass by the belief will solidify as you will show more resilience in dealing with criticism.

Atlast I want to end at a movie scene where a small hotel owner has a tussle with big businessman who threw shoes at him and that hotel owner use it as a evil eye and next time when that person cross by that hotel he gets amazed to see his shoes hanging and also the progress of hotel and ask his driver to stop his car nearby and visit the hotel and talk to the owner. hotel owner tell him that he used the shoe thrown at him as evil eye and his hotel has progressed so much from doing this. This make the businessman very guilty and jealous of his action. This is how you will become and deal with any shoes thrown by people and life at you in such a manner that it will become a thing in your favor. I wish you all the luck in your journey to develop a attitude to turn thrown stones into castles.

Author's Note

When I began writing about this about it is about letting know others how to deal with criticism along with telling them about importance about criticizing old social structures of the society. I want to write a short and crisp book which can make you aware and initiate a process and belief in yourself. I have been writing on an story telling app and the overwhelming response and love of people inspired me to write a book and this is my first book, i hope you would be considerate while evaluating it. When i was writing this book it was such an amazing experience for me, i would love to do it again. I always believe we need to rescue ourself. Every one of you has huge potential to become the best version of yourself and I believe you are already in that journey to your development. I love you all for what you are and what you are going to be. Keep reading and keep growing.

My mail mayankpawaiya007@gmail.com

Best wishes

Mayank Singh Pawaiya

9 798887 333489

Printed by Libri Plureos GmbH in Hamburg, Germany